Speak in a Week
Mandarin Chinese
Week Two

Original design by Donald S. Rivera
Illustrated by Julie Bradbury
Written by Dr. Shannon Shi

Published & distributed by

Penton Overseas, Inc.
Carlsbad, CA

Speak in a Week®
Chinese:
Week Two

Published and distributed by Penton Overseas, Inc., 1958 Kellogg Avenue, Carlsbad, CA 92008.

www.pentonoverseas.com

Contact publisher by phone at (800) 748-5804 or via email, info@pentonoverseas.com.

First printing 2006
ISBN 1-59125-660-7

Contents:

How to Use Speak in a Week:

Start with **Lesson Nine.** If you've studied Chinese before, you'll move on more quickly. Follow the lessons in order so you learn everything well. Master each lesson before you go to the next one.

Each lesson begins with an outline of what you'll be learning, followed by ten illustrated examples, first in Chinese, then in English. For every lesson, there's a track on the audio CD to help you with Chinese pronunciation.

On the illustrated pages, you'll also find extra grammar tips, helpful hints, and interesting facts about Chinese-speaking cultures. Following the eight lessons, you'll find a reference section with basic info, more words, and extra grammar.

When you've finished the lessons, go to the audio CD and listen to the last five tracks: **The Mastery Exercises.** You'll play with the Chinese you now know, so that you'll be able to make new sentences from what you've learned.

You'll be speaking Mandarin Chinese!

In this lesson you will learn . . .

- to ask questions using the words, *What?, Where?, When?, Who?, Why?, Which?, How?*, etc.

- to learn common phrases with question words:
  What is your name?
  Where is the restroom?
  When is your birthday?

- review the measure word 个 gè

In Chinese, there are nine important question words you have to know. Master the following words and you'll be able to get information about anyone and anything:

Who?	谁？	shéi
What?	什么？	shén me
Where?	哪儿？	nǎr
When?	什么时候？	shén me shí hòu
How?	怎么样/怎么？	zěn me yàng/zěn me
Why?	为什么？	wèi shén me
Which?	哪？	nǎ
How many?	多少？几？	duō shǎo, jǐ
How much?	多少？	duō shǎo

When a W-word, i.e. question word, is used in a question, its sentence structure is different from a regular one—there is no 吗 ma at the end of the question. Now compare: 你忙吗? nǐ máng ma (Are you busy?) 多少钱? duō shǎo qián (How much is it?)

怎么了?
zěn me le

怎么 zěn me means how or what. 了 le here works as a particle, indicating the change of the situation. Thus the phrase asks What happened? Please note both 么 me & 了 le have no tone marks, so you need to sound them light and quick.

3

What happened?

This phrase is often used when people sensed something wrong, or a change of the situation. It's a common way to show your concern or sympathy towards others.

4

几点了?
jǐ diǎn le

几 jǐ means how many and 点 diǎn o'clock. By putting them together, 几点 jǐ diǎn simply asks what time? Have you noticed that there is a total of four dots at the bottom of 点 diǎn? Make sure you get all of them when practicing writing.

What time is it?

Remember always use 点 diǎn (o'clock) to tell hours. For example, 3 o'clock is 三点 sān diǎn. Easy? Now go to Glossary Page 187 and practice!

6

你在哪儿工作?
nǐ zài nǎr gōng zuò

哪儿 nǎr, sometimes 哪里 nǎ lǐ, is used to ask Where? 哪儿 nǎr is colloquial and used in the North, and 哪里 nǎ lǐ is more formal and used in the South.

Where do you work?

This is one of the most common conversational questions you could ask. Often, people are proud of their work and have a lot to tell you.

8

这个多少钱?
zhè gè duō shǎo qián

多少 duō shǎo is how much? or How many?, and
钱 qián money. So all together 多少钱? duō shǎo
qián means How much money? 这个 zhè gè is this
one. Do you still remember what 个 gè is?
A "measure word"? Correct!

9

> **How much does it cost?**

You may just ask 多少钱? duō shǎo qián. Don't be afraid of bargaining. It is part of the Chinese culture. Enjoy interacting with people and practicing the phrases you learned at the same time!

你有多少?
nǐ yǒu duō shǎo

By itself, 多 duō actually means more and 少 shǎo means less, but when put together and used in a question, 多少 duō shǎo turns into how many? or how much?

11

How many do you have?

Interested in other foods? Go to Glossary Page 201-204. Now try this: how many biscuits do you have?

谁呀？
shéi ya

This is a commonly used phrase when people answer the door. 谁 shéi is who? and the character 呀 ya, just a sound without any concrete meaning. Note that 呀 ya doesn't have a tone mark, so make sure you sound it light and short.

13

Who is it?

Unlike who in English that has two forms: who and whom, 谁 shéi has only one. For pronouns, Chinese subjective/objective forms are always the same.

为 wèi means for and 什么 shén me means what? When placed together, 为什么 wèi shén me is for what? or why?

15

Are you wondering why you're studying Chinese?
我为什么学习中文？wǒ wèi shén me xué xí
zhōng wén? Keep studying and one day you'll
know how to answer it.

16

你从哪儿来?
nǐ cóng nǎr lái

Again, 哪儿 nǎr means where? Have you ever thought about the character 从 cóng which is placed just before 哪儿 nǎr? 从 is a character made of two identical symbols: 人 (human) with one following the other.

Where are you from?

Here is one way to answer this frequently asked question. You may say: 我从美国来。wǒ cóng měi guó lái (I'm from America).

火车什么时候开?
huǒ chē shén me shí hòu kāi

什么时候 shén me shí hòu is when? or what time?. 火 huǒ indicates fire and 车 chē a general term for vehicle. But don't get it wrong--火车 huǒ chē here means a train, not a fire engine.

> **When does the
> train leave?**

Even today 火车 huǒ chē still is the main
transportation for most Chinese. It's effective
and economical! Do you know that it takes only
10 hours to go from Beijing to Shanghai?

你要哪一个?
nǐ yào nǎ yí gè

When used all by itself, 哪 nǎ means which?
哪一个 nǎ yí gè is which one? Again, 个 gè is a
Chinese measure word.

21

Which one do you want?

To get yourself familiar with W-questions, go to Glossary Page 236-240.

Lesson 10

In this lesson you will learn . . .

- to talk about activities you *like* or *dislike*

  ☛ 喜欢 xǐ huan,
  不喜欢 bù xǐ huan

- to talk about activities you *would like* to do

  ☛ 我想要 wǒ xiǎng yào,
  我想 wǒ xiǎng

- to talk about actions

  ☛ 聊天 liáo tiān, 旅行 lǚ xíng,
  工作 gōng zuò, 看 kàn, etc.

- to learn new measure words

  ☛ 件 jiàn, a measure word used
  for most of the garment nouns
  杯 bēi, a cup of, a glass of,
  a measure word for drinks

Chinese Verbs
Because they don't have conjugation, all Chinese verbs are always in their infinitive form. The negative form is made by using 不 bù in front of a verb (except for the verb 有 yǒu, to have, as well as in past and perfect tenses).

Chinese Sentences
The language concepts in this lesson are divided into small blocks of words or phrases. The words in the upper left-hand corner, upper right-hand corner and in the picture, can be moved around to form new sentences. Treat each block as a whole. Also it's a good idea to keep Chinese sentence structure in mind:

subject + verb + object
subject + verb1 + verb2 + object
subject + verb1 + time word or preposition phrase + verb2 + object

我喜欢...
wǒ xǐ huan

和我的朋友
hé wǒ de péng you

聊天
liáo tiān

Use 和 hé when you are with someone. But remember to sandwich 和我的朋友 hé wǒ de péng you, the prepositional phrase, between 喜欢 xǐ huan (to like) and 聊天 liáo tiān (to chat).

25

I like. . .   **to talk**

with my friends.

Again, Chinese nouns don't have plurals. So even though you have a lot of friends, you still say 朋友 péng you (friend).

我喜欢... 　　　　　在八月
wǒ xǐ huan 　　　　　zài bā yuè

旅行。
lǚ xíng

Use 喜欢 xǐ huan to state what you like. To make
the sound of X, say sear in English, which without
the r sound is the closest to the sound of X. Also
note here 喜 xǐ used in double, 喜喜, is a lucky
symbol in Chinese weddings.

I like. . .   to travel

in August.

Chinese months are named in numbers, therefore, 八月 bā yuè is month no. 8. Interested in how other months are named? check out Glossary pg. 192.

28

我不喜欢...
wǒ bù xǐ huan

星期六
xīng qī liù

工作。
gōng zuò

Use 不 bù to express a negative feeling. It is always placed before a verb, adjective or adverb. Chinese use a lunar calendar and both sun and moon symbols are used in 星期 xīng qī (week). Can you figure them out? 日 rì (sun) and 月 yuè (moon).

29

I don't like. . .   to work

on Saturdays.

Chinese weekdays are named in numbers too. 星期六 xīng qī liù literally means the sixth day of the week. How many days do people work in a week in China now? Five! And in Hong Kong? Five and a half!

你喜欢... 看
nǐ xǐ huan kàn

爱情小说吗?
ài qíng xiǎo shuō ma

爱 ài is love and 情 qíng is passion, so 爱情 altogether means romance. 爱 ài was simplified in the 1950s. It used to be written as 愛 with a heart symbol 心 inside.

Do you like. . .   to read

romantic books?

The Chinese verb 看 kàn could means to read, to look at, to watch, to see and to visit, etc. Therefore, an eye symbol 目 is built into the character 看.

你喜欢... 打
nǐ xǐ huan dǎ

网球吗？
wǎng qiú ma

Use 打 dǎ when playing ball games except soccer.
There is a hand symbol 扌 in 打, which is widely
seen in action verbs.

Do you like. . .   to play

tennis?

What's the most popular sport in China? Table tennis! 乒乓球, pīng pāng qiú. The name comes from the sound when playing it.

24

我想要...
wǒ xiǎng yào

买一件
mǎi yí jiàn

丝绸衬衫。
sī chóu chèn shān

丝绸 sī chóu is silk and you actually can see 纟, the silk symbol on the left side of both characters. 件 jiàn is used here as a measure word for clothes and it untranslatable.

35

I would like. . .   to buy

a silk shirt.

Silk has been a traditional fabric in China for
thousands of years. It's still a top choice for
luxury and comfort today.

我想...
wǒ xiǎng

要
yào

宫保鸡丁。
gōng bǎo jī dīng

This is a typical sentence used to order food in a res-
taurant. 宫保 gōng bǎo is an ancient chef famous
for making hot & spicy dishes. Today, 宫保 gōng
bǎo has become a word for anything hot & spicy.

I would like. . .   to order

**Gong Bao
chicken.**

Where do you find the "hot & spicy" cuisine in
China? Sichuan & Hunan. That's right.
宫保 gōng bǎo happened to be a legendary
chef from Sichuan.

我想要... 七点
wǒ xiǎng yào qī diǎn

吃饭。
chī fàn

七点 qī diǎn means seven o'clock or at seven o'clock.
Time words such as 七点 qī diǎn always goes before
the action verb, which is 吃饭 chī fàn here. Go to
Glossary pg. 194 to learn more on time words.

39

I would like. . .   **to eat**

at seven o' clock.

Eat a comfortable breakfast in the morning,
a satisfying lunch at noon and a light dinner
in the evening – a Chinese secret for keeping
yourself in shape.

44

你想...
nǐ xiǎng

喝
hē

一杯绿茶吗?
yī bēi lǜ chá ma

茶 chá has two radicals: grass ⺾ and wood 木. That's because tea is made from the leaves of a tea shrub or tea tree. 杯 bēi (cup) here is a measure word (a cup of).

41

Would you like...   to have

a cup of green tea?

What's the national drink of China? Of course green tea! Although Chinese do drink other teas, for example, Wulong, Puer and Jasmine tea, green tea is always the favorite.

你想...
nǐ xiǎng

看
kàn

电影吗?
diàn yǐng ma

When silent movies were introduced in China in 1930s, Chinese called it electrical shadows, which is exactly what 电影 diàn yǐng means in Chinese.

Would you like. . . to see

a movie?

For more words on Entertainment, see Glossary pg. 216. If you are interested in trying other verbs, go to the Action Verbs section on Glossary pgs. 222-35.

Lesson 11

In this lesson you will learn . . .

- to talk about things you *need* to do

  ☞ 我需要 wǒ xū yào

- to talk about things other people *need* to do

  ☞ 他需要 tā xū yào,
     你们需要 nǐ men xū yào

- the subject pronouns *I, you, he, she, we, they,* etc.

  ☞ 我 wǒ, 你 nǐ, 他 tā,
     他们 tā men, etc.

- new measure words

  ☞ 封 fēng, a measure word for letters
     次 cì, a measure word for flight & train schedules
     家 jiā, a measure word for businesses like a store, bank, etc.

Before beginning this lesson, study the Chinese subject pronouns below:

Singular

I	我	wǒ
you	你	nǐ (informal)
you	您	nín (formal)
he	他	tā
she	她	tā

Plural

we	我们	wǒ men
you	你们	nǐ men (informal)
you	您们	nín men (formal)
they	他们	tā men
they	她们	tā men

Chinese pronouns do not have either masculine or feminine forms. For a group mixed with males and females, use the male plural, i.e. 他们 tā men (they).

我需要...
wǒ xū yào

准备
zhǔn bèi

考试。
kǎo shì

The two verbs used here, 需要 xū yào and 准备 zhǔn bèi are both in their infinitive form. In Chinese, you don't need to say "to prepare", just "prepare", if "prepare" is the second verb.

47

I need. . .   to study

for the exam.

准备 zhǔn bèi implies the "to prepare for", and that's why you don't see the Chinese equivalent of the English word for. Due to fierce competition nationwide, Chinese students today are still under

48

我需要... 去
wǒ xū yào qù

超市。
chāo shì

超 chāo here means super and 市 shì originated as a market and now it's also used as a town or city. Altogether, 超市 chāo shì means a super market. 去 qù implies "to go to".

49

I need. . .   **to go**

to the supermarket.

In China today, supermarkets are only available in large cities. In small towns and the countryside, people still go to their local grocery stores, or to an open-air market.

50

你需要...
nǐ xū yào

洗
xǐ

车。
chē

Use 洗 xǐ when you means to wash or clean. The radical, 氵, at the left of the character, is a water symbol. 车 chē is a simplified character and its traditional form is 車, which was created based on the shape of an ancient chariot.

You need. . . **to wash**

the car.

Time to do a little house cleaning? Go to Glossary pg. 207 to check out all the words you need on cleaning supplies.

你需要...
nǐ xū yào

带
dài

这么多东西吗?
zhè me duō dōng xi ma

吗 ma is a question marker. It's usually placed right before the question mark. But remember, W-word questions and some other special type questions don't use 吗 ma, only the question mark.

53

Do you need. . . **to bring**

so many things?

It looks like the lady needs the help of a 服务员 fú wù yuán (a porter). Hopefully, she remembers to give him a 小费 xiǎo fèi (a tip).

54

你需要... 付
nǐ xū yào fù

账单。
zhàng dān

账单 zhàng dān is a check or bill. The word 账 zhàng is made of two components. 贝 bèi, on the left, could also be used as an independent character, a symbol of a cowry shell. In ancient China, cowry shells were widely used as currency.

You need. . .   to pay

the check.

Nowadays, Chinese can pay their personal bills by either cash, credit cards or debit cards, but not checks. There are no personal checks in China.

他需要...
tā xū yào

休息
xiū xi

一会儿。
yí huìr

Have you noticed that Chinese verbs don't change form, even when the subject is in the third person singular? The verb 需要 xū yào stay the same whether the subject is plural or singular, the first person or the third.

He needs. . . to rest

a little.

Chinese love to take a long lunch break, especially in the hot summer. Some people even prefer to have a nap after lunch. Don't be surprised if you have a hard time to find people on a summer afternoon.

她需要... 写
tā xū yào xiě

一封信。
yì fēng xìn

封 fēng is a measure word specifically used for 信 xìn. Generally speaking, nouns in Chinese don't require a measure word unless a number is used to describe the noun, such as 一封信 (one letter) or 三杯茶, sān bēi chá (three cups of tea).

She needs. . .   to write

a letter.

Chinese letters used to be written vertically and from right to left. This is because characters were written on a bamboo strip in the ancient time, and dozens of strips were connected together to make a scroll – thus a book.

他们需要...
tā men xū yào

换
huàn

一百美元。
yì bǎi měi yuán

美元 měi yuán literally means American dollar. 美 měi is made of 羊 yáng on the top and 大 dà at the bottom. Ancient Chinesed believe that when a sheep was big and fat, it's beautiful, so the character means beautiful. But 美 here is the transliteration of America.

They need. . .   to exchange

**one hundred
dollars.**

Do you know the exchange rate between a U.S. dollar and a Chinese yuan? 1:8, which means you have a bigger purchasing power when you live in China.

您们需要... 坐
nín men xū yào zuò

第十二次列车。
dì shí èr cì liè chē

Use 坐 zuò when you take any kind of transportation. For example, 坐汽车 zuò qì chē,(to take a bus), 坐飞机 zuò fēi jī (to take a flight), 坐轮船 zuò lún chuán (to take a cruise).

You need. . . to take

34 Beijing
16 Xian
12 Shanghai

train number twelve.

To make an ordinal number is to put 第 dì in front
of the number. 第十二次 dì shí èr cì means
No. 12. 次 cì here is a measure word for trains,
but it is untranslatable.

我们需要...
wǒ men xū yào

找
zhǎo

一家银行。
yì jiā yín háng

The literal translation of 银行 yín háng is silver firm, which conducts financial activities in China for the last thousands of years. It gets its name from the currencies used back then, like silver, gold and copper.

We need. . .   to find

a bank.

Because we use number 一 yì (one), we have to use a measure word between the number and 银行 yín háng (bank). Here 家 jiā (family) indicates that all businesses, big or small, all started from a family business

Lesson 12

In this lesson you will learn . . .

- to talk about what you *want* to do ☛ 我想... wǒ xiǎng

- to talk about what other people *want* to do ☛ 他想... tā xiǎng, 你们想... nǐ men xiǎng, etc.

- new words of action to *study, take, listen, come, sell,* etc. ☛ 学习 xué xí, 倒 dào, 听 tīng, 来 lái, 卖 mài, etc.

Interested in learning more action words?
Go to Glossary pages 222-235.

Affirmative & Negative Forms of to *Want* to

Before and after this lesson, learn and revisit the forms of verb *to Want to*:

Affirmative			**Negative**		
I want	我想	wǒ xiǎng	I don't want	我不想	wǒ bù xiǎng
You want	你想	nǐ xiǎng	You don't want	你不想	nǐ bù xiǎng
He wants	他想	tā xiǎng	He doesn't want	他不想	tā bù xiǎng
She wants	她想	tā xiǎng	She doesn't want	她不想	tā bù xiǎng
We want	我们想	wǒ men xiǎng	We don't want	我们不想	wǒ men bù xiǎng
You want	你们想	nǐ men xiǎng	You don't want	你们不想	nǐ men bù xiǎng
They want	他们想	tā men xiǎng	They don't want	他们不想	tā men bù xiǎng
They want	她们想	tā men xiǎng	They don't want	她们不想	tā men bù xiǎng

Use 她们想 when the group has all females.
Use 他们想 if the group has all males or a mix.

我想...
wǒ xiǎng

学习
xué xí

汉语。
hàn yǔ

想 xiǎng is to say what a person wants and therefore there is a heart radical 心 placed at the bottom of the character. Chinese tradition has long believed that it is the human heart that does the thinking and reasoning, rather than the brain.

I want. . .   to learn

Chinese.

Among a few different ways to say Chinese language, the most common ones are 汉语 hàn yǔ and 中文 zhōng wén. The former refers to "the language of Han people" who counts for 92% of China's population and the latter simply means the language of Chinese.

我不想...
wǒ bù xiǎng

倒
dào

垃圾。
lā jī.

Use 不 bù to express a negative connotation and place it in front of the verb. The common radical 土 tǔ in both 垃 lā and 圾 jī means dirt, although in modern times dirt is no longer the major component of trash.

71

I don't want. . .   to take out

the trash.

Once the trash is out, why not fix a couple of broken things around the house. Go to pgs. 209-210 to check Tools & Materials.

你想...
nǐ xiǎng

听
tīng

音乐吗?
yīn yuè ma

To listen to in Chinese is 听 tīng. The character has been simplified. Interestingly, the traditional form has a radical of ear 耳, while the simplified one has a 口 (mouth).

73

Do you want. . .   **to listen**

to music?

Study tip: listen to Chinese radio stations, watch
Chinese TV channels or videos. It will help you
develop an ear for the tone, intonation and
sentence rhythm.

你想...
nǐ xiǎng

来
lái

我家吗?
wǒ jiā ma

When it comes to family, home or house, you can use the character 家 jiā. Here it implies both a house and a home. 我家 is the colloquial form of 我的家 (my home). 的 de is usually omitted if the noun after 的 is a human noun like 家 jiā or 妈妈 mama (mother_.

Do you want. . . to come

to my house?

Want to learn the words on family members?
Check out Glossary pgs. 199-200.

老王想... 卖
lǎo wáng xiǎng mài

他的小船。
tā de xiǎo chuán

Address your friends, colleagues and neighbors by their last name and add 老 lǎo (old) before the last name, if they're older than you. It's an old Chinese custom. 老 here also states respect and familiarity.

Old Wang wants... to sell

his boat.

To buy and to sell in Chinese are two very similar characters: 买卖 with two very similar sounds: mǎi mài. But both characters contain a same part 头 tóu (head or brain). Of course you have to be clear-headed in business.

小平想... 给她妈妈
xiǎo píng xiǎng gěi tā mā ma

寄一个包裹。
jì yí gè bāo guǒ

Chinese sentence structure alters a little bit, when it contains a prepositional phrase like 给她妈妈 gěi tā mā ma (to her mom). Instead of placed at the end of a sentence, the prepositional phrase goes after the verb 想 xiǎng. When read, it should be 小平想给她妈妈寄一个包裹。 xiǎo píng xiǎng gěi tā mā ma jì yí gè bāo guo.

79

Xiao Ping wants. . .   **to send**

a package to her mother.

个 gè here is a measure word for 包裹 bāo guǒ (package). Some Chinese nouns require a specific measure word. For everything else, use 个 gè.

他们想... 在游泳池
tā men xiǎng zài yóu yǒng chí

游泳。
yóu yǒng

Again the prepositional phrase 在游泳池 zài yóu yǒng chí (in a swimming pool) has to be put before the action verb 游泳 yóu yǒng (to swim) and after 想 xiǎng. The sentence should be 他们想在游泳池游泳。tā men xiǎng zài yóu yǒng chí yóu yǒng.

They want. . . to swim

in the pool.

Notice the water symbol 氵 contained in 游泳池 yóu yǒng chí? That's right. 游泳 means to swim and 池 a pond. What else could be the symbol here?

82

你们想...　　看
nǐ men xiǎng　kàn

电视吗?
diàn shì ma

Remember 吗 ma? A question marker always put before the question mark. 电视 diàn shì literally means electric seeing, similar to television, the long-distance seeing.

83

Do you want. . .   to watch

television?

The plural form of Chinese pronouns is 们 men.
It can be used for a pronoun of any person, the
first, second or third person. Since it's just a plural
form, there is no tone mark on its top.

我们想... 骑
wǒ mén xiǎng qí

自行车。
zì xíng chē

Chinese called it self-walking vehicle, 自行车 zì xíng chē, when it was imported to China early last century. However, the verb 骑 qí is an ancient word, meaning to ride a horse. 骑 even has a horse symbol in it: 马 mǎ.

85

We want... to ride

bicycles.

Many Chinese still love to ride their bikes to work. Can you say it in Chinese? 我骑自行车上班！ wǒ qí zì xíng chē shàng bān! (I ride a bicycle to work!)

86

我们不想...
wǒ men bù xiǎng

等到
děng dào

明天。
míng tiān

Due to its positive connotation (bright, wise, smart, clearness, etc.), 明 míng has been a popular character. 明天 míng tiān means tomorrow and could imply that tomorrow will be a better day.

We don't want. . .   to wait

until tomorrow.

It is essential to be able to express different time elements. Use Glossary pgs. 195-198 to learn to say today, yesterday, the day after tomorrow, etc.

Lesson 13

In this lesson you will learn . . .

- to talk about what you *have to* do

  ☞ 我得... wǒ děi,
  我必须... wǒ bì xū

- to talk about what other people *have to* do

  ☞ 他得... tā děi,
  你们必须... nǐ men bì xū,
  etc.

- new words of action *to get, clean, cut, rent, wait,* etc.

  ☞ 办 bàn, 打扫 dǎ sǎo,
  剪 jiǎn, 租 zū, 等 děng, etc.

Different Words Used to Express **Have to**

Several words are used to express the feeling **to have** to do things:

得 děi -- The most commonly used one and often used in a colloquial setting.

必须 bì xū – The more formal choice. It expresses the feeling of doing thing out of obligation and rules. It leaves very little room for negotiation.

非要 fēi yào – Often used in a question, especially when in doubt about whether something has to be done.

我得...
wǒ děi

办
bàn

签证。
qiān zhèng

得 děi is the simplest and most commonly used have to, while there are other words with similar meanings. Use 得 děi after a subject which could be people or things.

91

I have... to get

a Visa.

Get ready for Travel with Glossary pg. 218. While you're there, check In the Hotel with Glossary pgs. 213-214.

我得...
wǒ děi

给我的妻子
gěi wǒ de qī zi

打电话。
dǎ diàn huà

打电话 dǎ diàn huà (to make a call or to call), literally means to 打 dǎ (hit) 电话 diàn huà (a telephone). 给我的妻子 gěi wǒ de qī zi (to my wife), a prepositional phrase, has to be placed before the verb 打 dǎ.

93

I have. . .   to call

my wife.

Can you say, "I have to call my uncle," in
Chinese? If you don't know, now it's the time to
learn! Glossary pgs. 199-200 Family Members.

你必须...
nǐ bì xū

问一问
wèn yí wèn

你的妈妈。
nǐ de mā ma

Use 必须 bì xū when something has to be done due to a rule or tradition. Also bì xū is more formal than 得 děi. When used, bì xū is always placed after the subject.

You have. . .   to ask

your mother.

It sounds redundant when 问一问 wèn yí wèn is used, (to ask an asking, if literally translated). This type of verbal phrase emphasizes the informality and is commonly used in colloquial Chinese.

你非要...
nǐ fēi yào

作
zuò

功课吗?
gōng kè ma

Use 非要 fēi yào in a question when you're not sure if something has to be done. 功课 gōng kè usually refers to school work or some spiritual work that a monk has to do in a Buddhist temple.

Do you have. . .   to do

homework?

Want to do some homework? Well, study this book whether you're in line, on a break or during a commercial. Twenty minutes a day will do you a lot of good!

你们得... 等
nǐ men děi děng

一会儿。
yí huìr

Use 一会儿 yí huìr when you mean a very short period of time. The 儿 has a very quick and light r sound, which is typical in Beijing Mandarin.

You have to. . .   **wait**

for a while.

Keep this in mind: a time word indicating the
length of time is usually put after the verb.

100

她得...
tā děi

打扫
dǎ sǎo

客厅。
kè tīng

Noticed that dǎ and sǎo have something in common? That's right! A hand 扌 symbol or radical. That's because when cleaning, you have to use your hands.

She has to. . .   **clean**

the living room.

Mastery Exercise: He has to clean the kitchen.

他不得不...
tā bù dé bù

剪
jiǎn

草坪。
cǎo píng

When you have to do things that you hate to do,
use 不得不 bù dé bù. The first 不 bù is negative,
but the second one makes the meaning positive.
The bottom of 剪 jiǎn is a knife radical 刀 (to cut
or mow here).

103

He has to. . .   **cut**

the grass.

Maintaining a house is not easy. A lot of work needs to be done inside & outside. Look up The House on Glossary pg. 208.

你得...
nǐ děi

留下
liú xià

小费。
xiǎo fèi

Use 得 děi also when giving people sincere advice or suggestions. 小 xiǎo means small or little, and 费 fèi money. Have you noticed the shell (ancient money) radical 贝 at the bottom of 费?

You have to... leave

a tip.

China's tip culture is still to come yet, except in a few big cities. In some Western-style hotels or restaurants, the gratuity (tip) is normally included in your bill or check.

他们必须...
tā men bì xū

4月8号
sì yuè bā hào

出发。
chū fā

Since the date is fixed, you need to use 必须 bì xū.
April 8th could be written as 四月八号 sì yuè bā
hào, or 4 月 8 号, with 月 as the month and 号
the date. Please also note here that Chinese time
word (4 月 8 号) goes before the verb (出发).

They have to. . .   leave

April 8th.

Chinese are still using a dual calendar system:
The Chinese lunar calendar and Western calendar. Want to know more about how months are
called in Chinese? See Glossary 192.

我们必须... 　　租
wǒ men bì xū 　　zū

一个公寓。
yí gè gōng yù

租 zū could be a verb (to rent) or noun (the rent).
The left side of the character, 禾 pronounced as
hé, means crops. In ancient China, 禾 were used
as rent by peasants to pay for the land leased from
the landlords.

We have to. . . rent

an apartment.

公寓 gōng yù literally means public residences, either rented or owned. In big cites like Beijing or Shanghai, most people live in 公寓 due to the shortage of land.

In this lesson you will learn . . .

- to talk about what you *are going to* do

  ☞ 我要... 了 wǒ yào... le,
     我打算... wǒ dǎ suàn, etc.

- to talk about what other people *are going to* do

  ☞ 他要... 了 tā yào... le,
     你们打算... nǐ men dǎ suàn, etc

- new words of action *to turn on, sleep, visit, arrive, wear,* etc.

  ☞ 开 kāi, 睡 shuì,
     参观 cān guān, 到 dào,
     戴 dài, etc.

Different Words Used to Express **to be going to**

There are several words used when people **are going to** do things:

要... 了 yào... le -- The most commonly used one and often used in colloquial setting.

打算 dǎ suàn – Has less urgency than 要... 了. Also expresses the meaning of planning and scheduling.

要 yào – Often used to replace 要... 了. It's the simpler form of 要... 了.

我要...
wǒ yào

开
kāi

灯了。
dēng le

Use 要... 了 yào... le when you are going to do something very soon. 灯 dēng (lamp or light) has a radical of fire 火 huǒ, which was the main lighting in ancient time. If you're going to turn off the light, say: 我要关灯了 wǒ yào guān dēng le.

I am going to...   turn off

the light.

Use the verb 开 kāi when you turn on 电视 diàn shì (TV), 水龙头 shuǐ lóng tóu (a faucet), 煤气 méi qì (gas) or drive a 车 chē (a car).

114

你打算...
nǐ dǎ suàn

睡
shuì

一整天吗?
yì zhěng tiān ma

Besides meaning to be going to, the verb 打算 dǎ suàn also expresses the sense of planning. On the left side of the character 睡 shuì, there is an eye radical 目 mù. Of course, your eyes are closed when sleeping.

Are you going to. . .   sleep

all day?

Mastery Exercise: Are you going to study all day? Don't know the verb for study? Check out Glossary pgs. 222-235.

你们要...
nǐ men yào

参观
cān guān

那个寺庙吗?
nà gè sì miào ma

Another option to express to be going to is 要 yào. The verb 参观 cān guān could only be used to visit objects or things, never humans. For example, you can't say 参观你妈妈 (to visit your mom), even though the verb means to visit.

Are you going to. . .   **visit**

the temple?

If you like to travel, be sure to stop by the
Points of Interest on page 218.

118

他要... 他要晚点儿

晚点儿
tā yào

wǎn diǎnr

到。
dào

Time words can go either before or after a verb depending it's meaning. If it shows the length of time, put it after the verb. But if it states a specific time such as 晚点儿 wǎn diǎnr (late), place it before the verb: 他要晚点儿到.

He is going to. . .   arrive

late.

Mastery exercise: He is going to arrive at 5:15.
Need help? Go to Dates and Time, Glossary pgs.
193-198.

她要...
tā yào

戴
dài

她最心爱的帽子。
tā zuì xīn ài de mào zi

The verb 戴 dài can only go with hats, scarves, ties, glasses, wigs, and jewelry items. For clothing, socks and shoes, use the verb 穿 chuān. And perfume? Use 洒 sǎ.

121

She is going to. . . **wear**

her favorite hat.

Remember to use the audio CD to help you practice your pronunciation.

122

岩岩要...
yán yán yào

帮助
bāng zhù

他的姨妈。
tā de yí mā

Have you noticed that almost all the Chinese characters referring to females or female activities, always have a female radical 女 nǚ, such as 姨妈 yí mā (aunt) here.

Yan Yan is going to... help

his aunt.

Chinese love to call their kids by a double-sounded nick name, such as yan yan here. Even the names given for pandas follow the same pattern. It's a sign of love and joy!

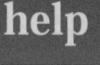

他们打算... 　　　　　　　跑
tā men dǎ suàn 　　　　　　pǎo

5 公里。
wǔ gōng lǐ

The Chinese verb 跑 pǎo has a built-in foot radical in it. Can you see it? The one on the left. That's right. 足 pronounced as zú, is a Chinese foot radical, which you can find in verbs like 跳 tiào (to jump), 踢 tī (to kick) and 踩 cǎi (to step).

They are going to. . .   run

5 kilometers.

A kilometer is 0.62 mile. Chinese uses metric system for length and weight, etc. See Portions and Measurements on Glossary pgs. 242-243.

你们打算...
nǐ men dǎ suàn

今天
jīn tiān

做完吗?
zuò wán ma

The verb 做 zuò by itself means to do or make. When used with 完 wán (to end or the end), it means that something is done. The time word 今 天 jīn tiān indicates a specific time, thus it should be put before the verb: 你们打算今天做完吗?

Are you going to... finish

today?

The character 完 wán is always seen on the screen at the end of a Chinese movie. When you see that word, you know the movie is done.

我们就要...
wǒ men jiù yào

经过
jīng guò

很多景点了。
hěn duō jǐng diǎn le

Use 就要...了 jiù yào... le as an alternative to express *is going to*. This structure has a more urgent sense than 打算 dǎ suàn and is often used to mean something is to happen really soon.

We are going to... pass

many points of interest.

The best time to travel in China, if your schedule allows, is spring and fall. The weather is the most pleasant and 景点 jǐng diǎn are much less crowded.

我们去...
wǒ men qù

看看
kàn kàn

旅游纪念品吧。
lǚ yóu jì niàn pǐn ba

Chinese verbs are often repeated in a sentence. It's colloquial and casual. 看看 kàn kàn (to take a look, to look for) expresses the feeling of window shopping or just checking it out.

Let's go. . .   look for

some souvenirs.

Want some souvenirs? Check out a mall
(购物中心 gòu wù zhōng xīn), a souvenir
store (旅游商店 lǚ yóu shāng diàn), or
street venders (地摊, dì tān).

In this lesson you will learn . . .

- to talk about what you are **able to / can** do
  - ☞ 我会... wǒ huì...,
    我可以... wǒ kě yǐ, etc.

- to talk about what other people are **able to / can** do
  - ☞ 他会... tā huì...,
    你们可以... nǐ men kě yǐ, etc.

- new words of action to **play, eat, wash, park, walk, use,** etc.
  - ☞ 弹 tán, 吃 chī, 洗 xǐ,
    停 tíng, 走 zǒu,
    用 yòng, etc.

Different Words Used to Express *to be able to / can*

Several words could be used when people are able to or can do things:

会... huì... -- shows the skills learned through education, apprenticeship and training;

能... néng... – often indicates to be able to "make it" or not due to certain circumstances;

可以.. kě yǐ... – Often used to ask or give permission; also used to make a request;

我会... 弹
wǒ huì tán

钢琴。
gāng qín

To play could be translated into quite a few
different Chinese verbs. 弹 tán is to play a musical
instrument with a keyboard, or some string instru-
ments using the fingers to play, such as a guitar or
Chinese Pi Ba.

I can. . .   play

piano.

会 huì is used to emphasize a skill acquired
through education, apprenticeship or training.
Now try this: I can speak Chinese!

(我会说中文! Wǒ huì shuō zhōng wén)

136

我可以...
wǒ kě yǐ

用
yòng

电话吗?
diàn huà ma

Use 可以 kě yǐ when you ask for permission to use or do things. To answer this question, you may use either 可以。kě yǐ (You may.) or 不可以。bù kě yǐ (You may not.)

Can I. . .   use

the telephone?

The Chinese way to answer a phone call is first to say 喂！wéi (Hello.) To ask the caller to hold on, say 请等一下。qǐng děng yí xià.

我不能...
wǒ bù méng

养
yǎng

狗。
gǒu

Use 能 méng when you can, or can't, make it due to certain circumstances. If having a dog would cause allergies, then the verb should be 不能 bù méng, instead of 不会 bú huì (skill) or 不可以 bù kě yǐ (permission).

139

I can't. . .   have

a dog.

If your pet 宠物 chǒng wù gets sick, you better take it to a 宠物医院 chǒng wù yī yuàn (a pet hospital).

140

他不能... 　　　　吃
tā bù néng 　　　　chī

辣椒。
là jiāo

See the mouth radical of the verb 吃? 口 kǒu is commonly used in characters related to using mouth, such as 喝 hē (to drink), 唱 chàng (to sing) and 叫 jiào (to be called).

He can't. . . eat

hot peppers.

Cultural quiz: what is the hottest and the spiciest cuisine of China?

(Sichuan and Hunan; Sichuan dishes also have a numbing effect.)

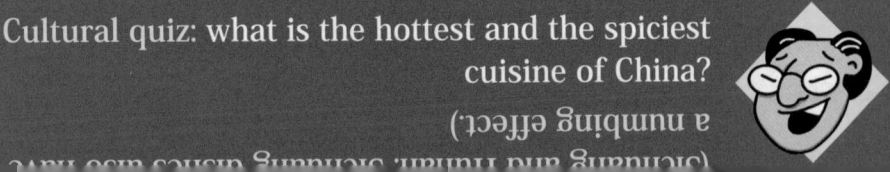

你可以...
nǐ kě yǐ

洗
xǐ

碗吗?
wǎn ma

可以 kě yǐ could also be used when asking others to do things for you. It shows a sense of respect and politeness. The chances are, if you ask politely, your request will be fulfilled!

Can you. . .   **wash**

the dishes?

Chinese use 碗 wǎn (a bowl) to eat, like Westerners use dishes. Plates & dishes are to hold meat, fish or vegetables on a Chinese dinner table.

你能... 开得
nǐ néng kāi de

慢一点吗?
màn yì diǎn ma

得 de is put between a verb and an adverb. 得 doesn't have a meaning of its own and no tone mark either. Use 得 when you want to describe an action such as 慢 màn (slowly) or 快 kuài (fast).

145

Can you. . .   drive

slower please?

Want to drive in China? Here's an important sign for you to know: 停 tíng (Stop). The left side 亻 is a human radical—Driver stop!

146

小刘不会...
xiǎo liú bú huì

打
dǎ

太极拳。
tài jí quán

In Chinese culture, a young man, or woman, in his/ her 20s or 30s, is often called by their last name plus 小 xiǎo (young), as in 小刘, 小王 xiǎo wáng (young Wang) or 小李 xiǎo lǐ (young Li).

Young Liu can't. . . do

Tai Ji.

You might know Tai Ji as Tai Qi. Well, the former is the standard Romanization pronunciation of 太极 and the latter, the Wade-Giles, is an older form.

他们会...
tā men huì

跳
tiào

拉丁舞。
lā dīng wǔ

拉丁 lā dīng comes from the word Latin. 舞 wǔ is a very complex character and never simplified. It was created to show a dancer's arms and legs moving all around.

They can. . .   dance

the Latin dance.

In China, people could learn 民族舞 mín zú wǔ (folk dance), 芭蕾舞 bā léi wǔ (ballet) or 交际舞 jiāo jì wǔ (ballroom dancing).

150

你能...
nǐ néng

走得
zǒu dé

快一点吗?
kuài yì diǎn ma

In Chinese, the meaning of being "faster", "nicer", "cheaper", etc. is expressed by adding a few words before or after the verb. You may use 一点 yì diǎn, 一些 yì xiē or 更 gèng.

151

Can you. . . walk faster?

Mastery Exercise: We have to walk faster.

(我们需要走得快一点。) wǒ men xū yào zǒu de
kuài yì diǎn)

152

我们可以... 在这儿
wǒ men kě yǐ zài zhèr

停车。
tíng chē

停 tíng by itself, means to stop and 停车 tíng chē to stop the car or park. Glad to see a parking space? Then say 我们可以在这儿停车。wǒ men kě yǐ zài zhèr tíng chē (Not 停车在这儿 tíng chē zài zhèr).

We can...   park

here.

Get ready to pay 停车费 tíng chē fèi (parking fee) after you find a spot in the 停车场 tíng chē chǎng (parking lot). Parking is always costly in China.

154

Lesson 16

In this lesson you will learn . . .

- review the *question words*:

  什么 shén me, 哪儿 nǎr, 多少 duō shǎo, 怎么 zěn me, etc.

- practice making questions out of the words and concepts from this lesson:

  吃什么 chī shén me, 怎么去北京 zěn me qù běi jīng, etc.

- use Glossary pages 236-241 with this lesson

155

You are on your way to becoming a master of Chinese.

Once you can use the concepts from this lesson, you will be well on your way to becoming a master at speaking Chinese. You still, however, need to review what you have learned so far.

Make great use of all the lessons, Glossary pages and the CD. Let the Chinese sound be with you all the time. Be honest with yourself and focus on building a strong foundation. Whenever you feel unsure, always go back and review.

Due to the difficulty of Chinese pronunciation, you're going to continue seeing pinyin with Chinese characters throughout the whole book!

你想玩什么？
nǐ xiǎng wán shén me

什么 shén me (what) is often placed at the end of a question. Because 什么 is a question word, the question with 什么 doesn't have 吗 ma at the end.

What do you want to play?

Whenever 你 nǐ is used, instead of 您 nín, the sentence is informal.

你想喝什么?
nǐ xiǎng hē shén me

Mastery Exercise: 你要吃什么?
nǐ yào chī shén me

What would you like to drink?

Mastery Exercise: What do you want to eat?

我应该什么时候回来?
wǒ yīng gāi shén me shí hòu huí lai

When 什么 shén me is used as part of the
什么时候 shén me shí hòu (what time? when?),
it goes before the verb.

When do I need to return?

Again because 什么时候 is a question-word, this kind of question doesn't have 吗 ma at the end.

162

我在哪儿能找到出租车？
wǒ zài nǎr néng zhǎo dào chū zū chē

Mastery Exercise: 我在哪儿能停车？
wǒ zài nǎr néng tíng chē

Where can I find a taxi?

Mastery Exercise: Where can I park?

164

你要换多少钱？
nǐ yào huàn duō shǎo qián

多少钱 duō shǎo qián (how much money) is the question-word here, so the sentence ends without 吗 ma.

How much do you want to exchange?

You may just ask 多少 duō shǎo without 钱 qián (money), in an informal setting.

你能看见几个?
nǐ néng kàn jiàn jǐ gè

You may also use 多少个 duō shǎo gè (how many) as an option to 几个 jǐ gè (how many).

How many can you see?

As a measure word (or counting word), 个 is usually used with a number or words like "多少". A measure word in Chinese sometimes is untranslatable.

168

你为什么不喜欢跳舞?

nǐ wèi shén me bù xǐ huān tiào wǔ

Mastery Exercise: 我为什么要倒垃圾?

wǒ wèi shén me yào dào lā jī

Why don't you like to dance?

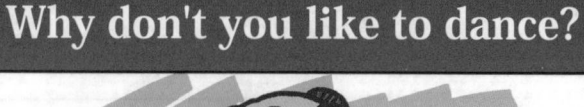

Mastery Exercise: Why do I have to take out the trash?

你要怎么付款?
nǐ yào zěn me fù kuǎn

Mastery Exercise: 你要怎么去北京?
nǐ yào zěn me qù běi jīng

How are you going to pay?

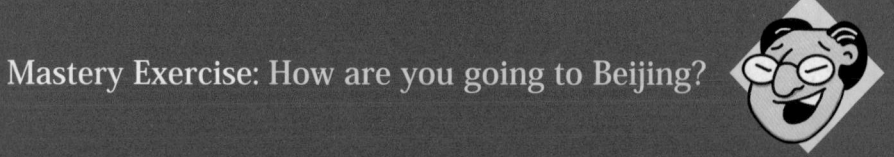

Mastery Exercise: How are you going to Beijing?

172

谁想上洗手间?
shéi xiǎng shàng xǐ shǒu jiān

Mastery Exercise: 谁想看电视?
shéi xiǎng kàn diàn shì

173

Who needs to go to the bathroom?

Mastery Exercise: Who wants to watch television?

174

你要买哪一个?
nǐ yào mǎi nǎ yí gè

Mastery Exercise: 你喜欢哪一个?
nǐ xǐ huan nǎ yí gè

Which one do you want to buy?

Mastery Exercise: Which one do you like?

Glossary

Glossary (cont.)

Chinese Phonetic Alphabet (pin yin)

a	n
b	o
c	p
d	q
e	r
f	s
g	t
h	u
i	v
j	w
k	x
l	y
m	z

The Chinese pinyin adopts the Latin alphabet. V is only used to spell foreign, minority or dialectic words.

Chinese Vowels

Vowel	Similar English sounds	Chinese	Pinyin
a	papa, mama	爸爸	bà ba
o	what	我	wǒ
e	about	河	hé
i	tea	李	lǐ
u	food	图	tú
ü		女	nǚ

Pinyin Consonants

Consonant	Similar English sounds	Chinese	Pinyin
b	**b**read	白 (white)	bái
p	**p**ope	平 (flat)	píng
m	**m**op	美 (pretty)	měi
f	**f**oot	风 (wind)	fēng
d	**d**ay	大 (big)	dà
t	**t**ie	天 (day)	tiān
n	**n**urse	男 (male)	nán
l	**l**ife	老 (old)	lǎo
g	**g**ood	工 (work)	gōng
k	**k**ey	口 (mouth)	kǒu
h	**h**at	好 (good)	hǎo

Pinyin Consonants

Consonant	Similar English sounds	Chinese	Pinyin
j	**jee**p	家 (home)	jiā
q	**chee**se	气 (air)	qì
x	**s**ea	下 (down)	xià
zh	**J**une	中 (middle)	zhōng
ch	**ch**urch	车 (car)	chē
sh	**sh**ow	上 (up)	shàng
r	televi**s**ion	人 (man)	rén
z	be**ds**	左 (left)	zuǒ
c	pan**ts**	草 (grass)	cǎo
s	**s**nake	三 (three)	sān

Special Rules of Chinese Sound

W - W is not a formal consonant in Chinese pinyin. However, when a sound starts with the vowel **u**, such as **u, ua, uo, uai, uei, uan, uen, uang, ueng,** and there is no consonant before it, the **u** is written as **w**.

Y - Y is not a formal consonant in Chinese pinyin. However, when a sound starts with the vowel **i**, such as **i, ia, ie, iao, iou, ian, in, iang, ing, iong,** and there is no consonant before it, the **i** is written as **Y**.

When a sound starts with the vowel **ü**, such as **ü, üe, üan, ün,** and there is no consonant before it, **Y** is added before **ü** and the umlaut is often omitted.

Tones

Chinese is a tonal language and has a total of four tones. The explanation of them is as follows:

Tone name	Tone mark	Explanation
1st tone	ā, ēi, ōng	flat
2nd tone	á, én, íng	up, rising
3rd tone	ǎi, ǒu, ěi	falling-rising
4th tone	ào, uè, èi	falling, down

If you have problems with tones, here's something you can try: John (flat). Are you coming (rising)? Well (falling-rising), yes (down). If a sound carries a soft, there is no tone mark for it. For example:

妈 (mā)　　麻 (má)　　马 (mǎ)　　骂 (mà)　　吗 (ma)

Punctuation

Chinese punctuation is used in the same way it is used in English, except:

。 The Chinese period is a little hollow circle, which is used after a complete sentence.

他有太阳镜。 (He has sunglasses.)

、 It is used when you're listing similar things.

我们想买咖啡、可乐、啤酒和茶。

(We want to buy coffee, soda, beer and tea.)

《 》 Is used when you mention the title of a book, journal, play, song or an article.

你们有《时代》周刊吗?

(Do you carry any Time magazine?)

Plural

In general, nouns in the Chinese language do not have plural forms. For example, 桌子 zhuō zi (table) in 一张桌子 yì zhāng zhuō zi (one table) remains the same as in 三张桌子 sān zhāng zhuō zi (three tables).

However, Chinese pronouns do have plurals. Here's how it works:

Pronoun Singular
我 wǒ (I, me)
你 nǐ (you, you)
他 tā (he, him)
她 tā (she, her)
它 tā (it, it)

Pronoun Plural
我们 wǒ men (we, us)
你们 nǐ men (you, you)
他们 tā men (they, them)
她们 tā men (they, them)
它们 tā men (they, them)

Numbers 0-9

0	零	líng
1	一	yī
2	二	èr
3	三	sān
4	四	sì
5	五	wǔ
6	六	liù
7	七	qī
8	八	bā
9	九	jiǔ

零 líng is often written as "0" to simplify the writing.

Numbers 10-19

10	十	shí
11	十一	shí yī
12	十二	shí èr
13	十三	shí sān
14	十四	shí sì
15	十五	shí wǔ
16	十六	shí liù
17	十七	shí qī
18	十八	shí bā
19	十九	shí jiǔ

For number 11 to 19, an alternative way is to put a 一 before 十, such as 一十, 一十一, ……一十九.

Numbers 20-99

20	二十	èr shí
21	二十一	èr shí yī
30	三十	sān shí
40	四十	sì shí
50	五十	wǔ shí
60	六十	liù shí
70	七十	qī shí
80	八十	bā shí
90	九十	jiǔ shí
99	九十九	jiǔ shí jiǔ

Numbers 100-1,000,000

100	一百	yì bǎi
101	一百零一	yì bǎi líng yī
200	二百	èr bǎi
500	五百	wǔ bǎi
700	七百	qī bǎi
900	九百	jiǔ bǎi
1,000	一千	yì qiān
100,000	十万	shí wàn
1,000,000	一百万	yì bǎi wàn

Days of the Week

Monday	星期一	xīng qī yī
Tuesday	星期二	xīng qī èr
Wednesday	星期三	xīng qī sān
Thursday	星期四	xīng qī sì
Friday	星期五	xīng qī wǔ
Saturday	星期六	xīng qī liù
Sunday	星期天	xīng qī tiān

China runs the same weekly calendar, i.e. five working days and a two-day weekend, as the Western world. The Chinese calendar starts its week on Monday.

There are two ways to say "Sunday": 星期天 xīng qī tiān or 星期日 xīng qī rì.

One colloquial way to say "week" is 礼拜 lǐ bài, meaning "to pray". You may say 礼拜一 lǐ bài yī, 礼拜二 lǐ bài èr, etc.

Months of the Year

January	一月	yī yuè
February	二月	èr yuè
March	三月	sān yuè
April	四月	sì yuè
May	五月	wǔ yuè
June	六月	liù yuè
July	七月	qī yuè
August	八月	bā yuè
September	九月	jiǔ yuè
October	十月	shí yuè
November	十一月	shí yī yuè
December	十二月	shí èr yuè

China uses a lunar calendar concurrently with a Western calendar, but the official dates and state affairs are always conducted and recorded according to the Western calendar.

Dates and Large Numbers

To express a specific date or time of an event, you simply use the days, months you already know. However, a Chinese year is expressed out differently than a large number.

For example, the year of 1998 is expressed as 一九九八 yī jiǔ jiǔ bā. You have to read each number one by one. While for the number 1,998, you say 一千九百九十八 yì qiān jiǔ bǎi jiǔ shí bā.

To express the date July 4, 1963, you use:

the year + the month + the date

一九六三年七月四号 yī jiǔ liù sān nián qī yuè sì hào

To express the year you were born, you use:

我生在... wǒ shēng zài...

(I was born in .....)

我生在一九七五年。 wǒ shēng zài yī jiǔ qī wǔ nián

(I was born in 1975.)

It is a custom to always have 年 nián (year) to go with the number such as 一九七五年 yī jiǔ qī wǔ nián.

What Time Is It?

What time is it?	几点了？	jǐ diǎn le?
It's 1:00.	一点。	yì diǎn
It's 2:00.	两点。	liǎng diǎn
It's 12:04.	十二点 0 四。	shí èr diǎn líng sì
It's 1:55.	一点五十五。	yì diǎn wǔ shí wǔ
It's 2:50. (less)	差十分三点。	chà shí fēn sān diǎn
It's 1:15. (a quarter)	一点一刻。	yì diǎn yí kè
It's 6:45. (3 quarters)	六点三刻。	Liù diǎn sān kè
It's 2:30. (half)	两点半。	liǎng diǎn bàn
1:00 sharp	一点正	yì diǎn zhěng
in one hour	一小时以后	yì xiǎo shí yǐ hòu
an hour ago	一小时以前	yì xiǎo shí yǐ qián

Time Elements

today	今天	jīn tiān
in the morning	早上	zǎo shàng
in the afternoon	下午	xià wǔ
in the evening	晚上	wǎn shàng
this morning	今天早上	jīn tiān zǎo shàng
this afternoon	今天下午	jīn tiān xià wǔ
tonight	今天晚上	jīn tiān wǎn shàng
on the dot	正点	zhèng diǎn
noon	中午	zhōng wǔ
as soon as possible	尽快	jìn kuài
just a minute	等一下	děng yí xià

Time Elements (Cont.)

tomorrow	明天	míng tiān
the day after tomorrow	后天	hòu tiān
yesterday	昨天	zuó tiān
the day before yesterday	前天	qián tiān
last night	昨天晚上	zuó tiān wǎng shàng
this week	这个星期	zhè ge xīng qī
last week	上个星期	shàng ge xīng qī
each week	每个星期	měi ge xīng qī
next week	下个星期	xià ge xīng qī
the weekend	周末	zhōu mō

Time Elements (Cont.)

a moment	一会儿	yí huìr
after	以后	yǐ hòu
all the time	始终	shǐ zhōng
always	总是	zǒng shì
before	以前	yǐ qián
during	在...时候	zài...shí hòu
early	早	zǎo
everyday	每天	měi tiān
late	晚	wǎn
later	以后	yǐ hòu
lots of times	多次	duō cì

Time Elements (Cont.)

never	从不	cóng bù
now	现在	xiàn zài
often	常常	cháng cháng
once	一次	yí cì
right now	立刻	lì kè
seldom	偶尔	ǒu ěr
since	自从	zì cóng
sometimes	有时	yǒu shí
soon	不久	bù jiǔ
frequently	频繁	pín fán
lately, recently	最近	zuì jìn
until	直到	zhí dào

Family Members

father	爸爸	bà ba
mother	妈妈	mā ma
son	儿子	ér zi
daughter	女儿	nǚ ér
elder brother	哥哥	gē ge
younger brother	弟弟	dì di
elder sister	姐姐	jiě jie
younger sister	妹妹	mèi mei
grandfather (father's side)	爷爷	yé ye
grandmother (father's side)	奶奶	nǎi nai
grandfather (mother's side)	姥爷	lǎo ye
grandmother (mother's side)	姥姥	lǎo lao

Chinese kinship is more complicated than that of most Western cultures. For example, the grandfather and grandmother on the mother's side are called differently than those on the father's side.

Family Members (Cont.)

elder cousin (male)	表哥	biǎo gē
younger cousin (male)	表弟	biǎo dì
elder cousin (female)	表姐	biǎo jiě
younger cousin (female)	表妹	biǎo mèi
nephew (father's side)	侄子	zhí zi
nephew (mother's side)	外甥	wài sheng
niece (father's side)	侄女	zhí nü
niece (mother's side)	外甥女	wài sheng nü
baby	婴儿	yīng ér
child	小孩儿	xiǎo háir
husband	丈夫	zhàng fu
wife	妻子	qī zi

Bread, Grains and Cereals

the food	食物	shí wù
bread	面包	miàn bāo
biscuit	小点心	xiǎo diǎn xīn
cereal	早餐麦片	zǎo cān mài piàn
cornbread	玉米糕	yǜ mǐ gāo
crackers	饼干	bǐng gān
crescent roll	牛角面包	niú jiǎo miàn bāo
French bread	法国面包	fǎ guó miàn bāo
muffin	松饼	sōng bǐng
toast	烤面包片	kǎo miàn bāo piàn
oatmeal	燕麦片	yàn mài piàn
bread w/ butter & jam	黄油果酱面包	huáng yóu guǒ jiàng miàn bāo

Dairy Products

butter	黄油	huáng yóu
cheese	奶酪	nǎi lào
cottage cheese	干酪	gān lào
cream cheese	奶油干酪	nǎi yóu gān lào
cream	奶油	nǎi yóu
sour cheese	酸奶酪	suān nǎi lào
whipped cream	生奶油	shēng nǎi yóu
eggs	鸡蛋	jī dàn
margarine	人造黄油	rén zào huáng yóu
omelet	煎蛋卷	jiān dàn juǎn
milk	牛奶	niú nǎi
yogurt	酸奶	suān nǎi

Ingredients and Condiments

broth	肉汤	ròu tāng
cinnamon	桂皮	guì pí
condiments	调味品	tiáo wèi pǐn
flour	面粉	miàn fěn
garlic	大蒜	dà suàn
honey	蜂蜜	fēng mì
ingredients	配料	pèi liào
jam/jelly	果酱	guǒ jiàng
mayonnaise	蛋黄酱	dàn huáng jiàng
mint	薄荷	bò he
mustard	芥末	jiè mo
nuts	干果	gān guǒ

Ingredients and Condiments (Cont.)

olive oil	橄榄油	gǎn lǎn yóu
pepper	胡椒	hú jiāo
salt	盐	yán
sauce	调味酱	tiáo wèi jiàng
sesame oil	香油	xiāng yóu
shortening	起酥油	qǐ sū yóu
soy sauce	酱油	jiàng yóu
spices	香料	xiāng liào
sugar	糖	táng
syrup	糖浆	táng jiāng
vanilla	香草	xiāng cǎo
vinegar	醋	cù

Containers

bag	袋子	dài zi
basket	篮子	lán zi
bottle	瓶子	píng zi
box	盒子	hé zi
bucket	桶	tǒng
can	罐头	guàn tou
carton	硬纸盒	yìng zhǐ hé
jar	罐子	guàn zi
package	包裹	bāo guǒ
paper	纸	zhǐ
plastic	塑料	sù liào

Appliances

blender	果汁机	guǒ zhī jī
can opener	开罐器	kāi guàn qì
dishwasher	洗碗机	xǐ wǎn jī
dryer	烘干机	hōng gān jī
freezer	冷冻机	lěng dòng jī
mixer	搅拌机	jiǎo bàn jī
oven	烤箱	kǎo xiāng
refrigerator	冰箱	bīng xiāng
rice cooker	米饭煲	mǐ fàn bǎo
stove	炉灶	lú zào
vacuum cleaner	吸尘器	xī chén qì
washing machine	洗衣机	xǐ yī jī

The Laundry

the laundry	脏衣服	zāng yī fu
broom	笤帚	tiáo zhou
detergent	洗衣粉	xǐ yī fěn
dry clean	干洗	gān xǐ
dustpan	簸箕	bò ji
hangers	衣架	yī jià
iron	熨斗	yùn dǒu
ironing board	烫衣板	tàng yī bǎn
mop	拖把	tuō bǎ
soap	肥皂	féi zào
sponge	海绵	hǎi mián
stain	污垢	wū gòu
starch	上浆	shàng jiāng

Patio and Garden

the patio	院子	yuàn zi
barbecue	烤肉炉	kǎo ròu lú
bee	蜜蜂	mì fēng
butterfly	蝴蝶	hú dié
flowers	鲜花	xiān huā
fountain	喷泉	pēn quán
garden	花园	huā yuán
grass	草	cǎo
insects	昆虫	kún chóng
lawn	草坪	cǎo píng
pool	游泳池	yóu yǒng chí
shrub	灌木	guàn mù
tree	树	shù

Tools and Materials

ax	斧子	fǔ zi
cement	水泥	shuǐ ní
cord (electric)	电线	diàn xiàn
drill	电钻	diàn zuàn
flashlight	手电筒	shǒu diàn tǒng
glue	胶水	jiāo shuǐ
hammer	锤子	chuí zi
hoe	锄头	chú tou
hose	水管	shuǐ guǎn
jack	插座	chā zuò
ladder	梯子	tī zi
level	水平仪	shuǐ píng yí

Tools and Materials (Cont.)

nails	钉子	dīng zi
paint	油漆	yóu qī
pliers	钳子	qián zi
rake	耙子	pá zi
saw	锯	jù
screw	螺丝钉	luó sī dīng
screw driver	改锥	gǎi zhuī
shovel	铁锨	tiě xiān
tape measure	卷尺	juǎn chǐ
tools	工具	gōng jù
wheelbarrow	手推车	shǒu tuī chē
wrench	扳手	bān shǒu

The Restaurant

appetizers	开胃菜	kāi wèi cài
bar	酒吧	jiǔ bā
breakfast	早饭	zǎo fàn
check	账单	zhàng dān
cook	厨师	chú shī
dim sum	小吃	xiǎo chī
dinner	晚饭	wǎn fàn
lunch	午饭	wǔ fàn
menu	菜单	cài dān
reservation	订位	dìng wèi
tip	小费	xiǎo fèi
waiter	服务员	fú wù yuán

Who's Calling

Hello!	Wéi?
Hello!	Nǐ hǎo!
Who's calling?	Nǎ yí wèi?
I'd like to speak to...	Wǒ yào zhǎo...
Can I speak with...	Wǒ xiǎng zhǎo...
Is Maria in?	Mǎ lì ya zài ma?
When will she return?	Tā shén me shí hòu huí lai?
Don't hang up!	Bié guà diàn huà!
Hold on please.	Qǐng děng yí xià.
May I leave a message?	Wǒ yào liú yan, kě yǐ ma?
I'll call back.	Wǒ zài dǎ huí lai.
Call me back.	Gěi wǒ huí diàn huà.

In The Hotel

Where is ...?	... 在哪儿?	... zài nǎr
the bellboy	服务员	fú wù yuán
the concierge	门房	mén fáng
the doorman	看门人	kān mén rén
the elevator	电梯	diàn tī
the floor	层	céng
the key	钥匙	yào shi
the maid	清洁工	qīng jié gōng
the manager	经理	jīng lǐ
the lobby	大堂	dà táng
the pool	游泳池	yóu yǒng chí

In The Hotel (Cont.)

English	Chinese	Pinyin
I need...	我要...	wǒ yào
a blanket	一条毯子	yì tiáo tǎn zi
a pillow	一个枕头	yí gè zhěn tou
a room	一个房间	yí gè fáng jiān
... single	一个单人间	yí gè dān rén jiān
... double	一个双人间	yí gè shuāng rén jiān
a sheet	一条床单	yì tiáo chuáng dān
a shower	一个洗澡间	yí gè xǐ zǎo jiān
more ice	再要一些冰	zài yào yì xiē bīng
more soap	再要一些肥皂	zài yào yì xiē féi zào
more towels	再要几条毛巾	zài yào jǐ tiáo máo jīn
toilet paper	卫生纸	wèi shēng zhǐ

In The Classroom

the classroom	教室	jiào shì
books	书	shū
chalk	粉笔	fěn bǐ
chalkboard	黑板	hēi bǎn
crayons	蜡笔	là bǐ
homework	作业	zuò yè
map	地图	dì tú
notebook	笔记本	bǐ jì běn
problems	问题	wèn tí
pupil's desk	课桌	kè zhuō
student	学生	xué sheng
teacher	老师	lǎo shī

Games and Toys

toys	玩具	wán jù
cards	扑克牌	pú kè pái
checkers	跳棋	tiào qí
chess	国际象棋	guó jì xiàng qí
doll	洋娃娃	yáng wá wa
games	游戏	yóu xì
kite	风筝	fēng zhen
marbles	弹球	tán qiú
puzzle	拼图游戏	pīn tú yóu xì
seesaw	翘翘板	qiào qiào bǎn
slide	滑梯	huá tī
swing	秋千	qiū qiān

Directions and Locations

over there	在那边	zài nà bian
straight ahead	一直往前	yì zhí wàng qián
anywhere	任何地方	rèn hé dì fang
everywhere	到处	dào chù
nowhere	哪里也没有	nǎ lǐ yě méi yǒu
somewhere	某个地方	mǒu gè dì fang
to the east	东边	dōng bian
to the west	西边	xī bian
to the north	北边	běi bian
to the south	南边	nán bian
to the right	右边	yòu bian
to the left	左边	zuǒ bian

Points of Interest

aquarium	水族馆	shuǐ zú guǎn	**beach**	海滩	hǎi tān
jungle	热带雨林	rè dài yǔ lin	**museum**	博物馆	bó wù guǎn
castle	城堡	chéng bǎo	**ocean**	海洋	hǎi yáng
cathedral	大教堂	dà jiào táng	**palace**	宫殿	gōng diàn
church	教堂	jiào táng	**park**	公园	gōng yuán
circus	马戏团	mǎ xì tuán	**ruins**	古迹	gǔ jī
city	城市	chéng shì	**stadium**	体育场	tǐ yù chǎng
concert	音乐会	yīn yuè huì	**square**	广场	guǎng chǎng
country	乡下	xiāng xià	**statue**	雕像	diāo xiàng
disco	迪斯科	dí sī kē	**the king**	国王	guó wáng
fair	自由市场	zì yóu shì chǎng	**the queen**	王后	wáng hòu
fountain	喷泉	pēn quán	**theater**	戏院	xì yuàn

Survival Phrases

Can you help me?	nǐ bāng yì bāng wǒ, hǎo ma
How do you say it?	zhè gè zěn me shuō
How do you spell it?	zhè gè zěn me xiě
I don't understand.	wǒ bù dǒng
Do you understand?	nǐ dǒng ma
Speak slower.	shuō màn yì diǎn
Where is the bathroom?	xǐ shǒu jiān zài na
Where are you from?	nǐ cóng nǎ lái
Excuse me!	duì bu qǐ
May I come in?	wǒ kě yǐ jìn lai ma
I need to find ...	wǒ yào zhǎo...
Help!	Jiù mìng ah

Common Phrases

Good for you!	duì nǐ yǒu hǎo chù
Really?	zhēn de
I think so.	wǒ xiǎng shì zhè yàng
I hope so.	xī wàng rú cǐ
I'm coming.	wǒ lái le
I'm going.	wǒ qù le
He/she has gone (left).	tā zǒu le
Of course.	dāng rán
Sure.	méi wèn tí
Just a minute.	děng yí xià
As a matter of fact...	shì shí shàng
Finally... (At last...)	zuì hòu

Common Phrases (Cont.)

More or less.	duō shǎo yǒu diǎn
Maybe.	kě néng
As usual.	yí guàn rú cǐ
From today on...	cóng jīn tiān kāi shǐ
Me too.	wǒ yě rú cǐ
Me neither.	wǒ yě bù
I'm very sorry.	hěn duì bu qǐ
In my opinion...	zài wǒ kàn lái
It's a deal!	hěn huá suàn
It's almost the time.	shí jiān kuài dào le
Above all...	zhǒng zhī...
It seems to me that...	wǒ rèn wéi...

Action Words (verbs)

abandon	放弃	fàng qì		**anger**	生气	shēng qì
absorb	吸收	xī shōu		**annul**	取消	qǔ xiāo
accept	接受	jiē shòu		**answer**	回答	huí dá
acquire	获得	huò dé		**appear**	出现	chū xiàn
add	增加	zēng jiā		**argue**	争论	zhēng lùn
adhere	坚持	jiān chí		**arrange**	安排	ān pái
adjust	调整	tiáo zhěng		**arrest**	逮捕	dài bǔ
advance	提前	tí qián		**ask**	问	wèn
advise	劝告	quàn gào		**ask for**	请求	qǐng qiú
affirm	肯定	kěn dìng		**assist**	帮助	bāng zhù
agree	同意	tóng yì		**attack**	攻击	gōng jī
analyze	分析	fēn xi		**attend**	参加	cān jiā

Action Words (verbs) Cont.

attract	吸引	xī yǐn	bite	咬	yǎo
authorize	授权	shòu quán	blame	责怪	zé guài
be	是	shì	bleed	流血	liú xuè
be able to	能够	néng gòu	block	阻挠	zǔ náo
be born	出生	chū shēng	blow	吹	chuī
be worth	价值	jià zhí	boil	煮开	zhǔ kāi
beat	打	dǎ	bother	打搅	dǎ jiǎo
beg	乞求	qǐ qiú	break	打破	dǎ pò
begin	开始	kāi shǐ	breathe	呼吸	hū xī
believe	相信	xiāng xìn	bring	带来	dài lái
bend	弯折	wēn zhé	build	建造	jiàn zào
bet	打赌	dǎ dǔ	burn	烧	shāo

Action Words (verbs) Cont.

consist	和...一致	hé...yí zhì	**cross**	交叉	jiāo chā
consult	请教	qǐng jiào	**cry**	哭	kū
contain	包含	bāo hán	**cure**	治愈	zhì yù
contribute	贡献	gòng xiàn	**cut**	割破	gē pò
control	控制	kòng zhì	**dance**	跳舞	tiào wǔ
converse	谈话	tán huà	**decide**	决定	jué dìng
convince	说服	shuō fú	**declare**	宣布	xuān bù
cook	烹调	pēng tiáo	**dedicate**	致力	zhì lì
correct	改正	gǎi zhèng	**defend**	防卫	fáng wèi
cost	花费	huā fèi	**delay**	推迟	tuī chí
cough	咳嗽	ké sou	**deliver**	递送	dì sòng
crash	碰撞	pèng zhuàng	**deny**	否认	fǒu rèn

Action Words (verbs) Cont.

English	中文	Pinyin	English	中文	Pinyin
depend	依靠	yī kào	**divide**	分开	fēn kāi
describe	描述	miáo shù	**do**	做	zuò
destroy	毁灭	huǐ miè	**draw**	画	huà
detain	拘留	jū liú	**dream**	做梦	zuò mèng
die	死	sǐ	**drink**	喝	hē
dig	挖	wā	**drive**	开车	kāi chē
direct	指示	zhǐ shì	**dry**	干燥	gān zào
discover	发现	fā xiàn	**earn**	挣	zhèng
discuss	讨论	tǎo lùn	**eat**	吃	chī
dissolve	解决	jiě jué	**eliminate**	排除	pái chú
distract	转移	zhuǎn yí	**empty**	倒空	dào kōng
distribute	分发	fēn fā	**end**	结束	jié shù

Action Words (verbs) Cont.

English	Chinese	Pinyin
enter	进入	jìn rù
escape	逃避	táo bì
evacuate	疏散	shū sàn
enjoy	享受	xiǎng shòu
examine	检查	jiǎn chá
exchange	交换	jiāo huàn
exist	存在	cún zài
explain	解释	jiě shì
explore	探险	tàn xiǎn
fall	摔倒	shuāi dǎo
fear	害怕	hài pà
feed	喂	wèi

English	Chinese	Pinyin
feel	觉得	jué de
fight	打架	dǎ jià
fill	填满	tián mǎn
find	寻找	xún zhǎo
finish	完成	wán chéng
fish	钓鱼	diào yú
fit	适合	shì hé
fix	解决	jiě jué
flee	逃跑	táo pǎo
fly	飞	fēi
follow	跟随	fēn suí
forbid	禁止	jìn zhǐ

Action Words (verbs) Cont.

forget	忘记	wàng jì	grow	生长	shēng zhǎng
forgive	原谅	yuán liàng	guess	猜测	cāi cè
form	形成	xíng chéng	hang	挂	guà
freeze	冷冻	lěng dòng	happen	发生	fā shēng
frighten	吓唬	xià hu	hate	恨	hèn
fulfill	完成	wán chéng	have	有	yǒu
function	运行	yùn xíng	have to	不得不	bù dé bù
get	获得	huò dé	hear	听	tīng
give	给	gěi	help	帮助	bāng zhù
go	去	qù	hide	躲藏	duǒ cáng
grab	抓	zhuā	hire	雇用	gù yòng
greet	问候	wèn hòu	hit	打	dǎ

Action Words (verbs) Cont.

hold	拿着	ná zhe	**insure**	确保	què bǎo
hug	拥抱	yōng bào	**install**	安装	ān zhuāng
imagine	想象	xiǎng xiàng	**interpret**	解释	jiě shì
include	包括	bāo kòu	**introduce**	介绍	jiè shào
increase	增加	zēng jiā	**invest**	投资	tóu zī
indicate	表示	biǎo shì	**investigate**	调查	diào chá
inflate	膨胀	péng zhàng	**invite**	邀请	yāo qǐng
inform	通知	tōng zhī	**judge**	审理	shěn lǐ
inhibit	抑制	yì zhì	**jump**	跳	tiào
injure	伤害	shāng hài	**keep**	保持	bǎo chí
insert	插入	chā rù	**kick**	踢	tī
inspect	检查	jiǎn chá	**kiss**	吻	wěn

Action Words (verbs) Cont.

know	知道	zhī dào	look	看	kàn
lay	放下	fàng xià	loosen	放松	fàng sōng
lead	带领	dài lǐng	lose	丢失	diū shī
leave	离开	lí kāi	love	爱	ài
lend	借给	jiè gěi	maintain	维修	wéi xiū
let	让	ràng	make	做	zuò
lie	说谎	shuō huǎng	mean	意思是	yì si shì
lift	提起	tí qǐ	measure	测量	cè liáng
light	照亮	zhào liàng	meet	见面	jiàn miàn
like	喜欢	xǐ huan	melt	融化	róng huà
listen	听	tīng	move	移动	yí dòng
live	住	zhù	name	命名	mìng míng

Action Words (verbs) Cont.

need	需要	xū yào	**offer**	提出	tí chū
neglect	忽视	hū luè	**omit**	省略	shěng luè
note	注意	zhù yì	**open**	打开	dǎ kāi
notify	通知	tōng zhī	**operate**	操作	cāo zuò
obey	服从	fú cóng	**oppose**	反对	fǎn duì
oblige	迫使	pò shǐ	**order**	命令	mìng lìng
observe	观察	guān chá	**owe**	欠	qiàn
obstruct	妨碍	fáng ài	**park**	停车	tíng chē
obtain	获得	huò dé	**pay**	付钱	fù qián
occupy	占领	zhàn lǐng	**perceive**	感到	gǎn dào
occur	发生	fā shēng	**permit**	允许	yún xǔ
offend	冒犯	mào fàn	**persist**	坚持	jiān chí

Action Words (verbs) Cont.

English	Chinese	Pinyin	English	Chinese	Pinyin
pick up	捡起	jiǎn qǐ	**progress**	进步	jìn bù
plant	种	zhòng	**prohibit**	禁止	jìn zhǐ
play	玩	wán	**promise**	许诺	xǔ nuò
plunge in	跳入	tiào rù	**propose**	建议	jiàn yì
point out	指出	zhǐ chū	**protect**	保护	bǎo hù
practice	练习	liàn xí	**prove**	证明	zhèng míng
pray	祷告	dǎo gào	**pull**	拉	lā
prefer	更喜欢	gèng xǐ huan	**push**	推	tuī
prepare	准备	zhǔn bèi	**put**	放	fàng
present	提出	tí chū	**quit**	辞职	cí zhí
prevent	预防	yù fáng	**reach**	到达	dào dá
proceed	进行	jìn xíng	**read**	读	dú

Action Words (verbs) Cont.

receive	收到	shōu dào	respond	回答	huí dá
recognize	认可	rèn kě	rest	休息	xiū xi
recover	恢复	huī fù	retire	退休	tuì xiū
reduce	减少	jiǎn shǎo	return	回来	huí lái
refer	提及	tí jí	ride	骑	qí
remember	记得	jì de	rob	抢	qiǎng
rent	租	zū	run	跑	pǎo
repair	修理	xiū lǐ	save	保存	bǎo cún
repeat	重复	chóng fù	say	说	shuō
require	要求	yāo qiú	scratch	刮	guā
resolve	解决	jiě jué	search	寻找	xún zhǎo
respect	尊敬	zūn jìng	see	看	kàn

Action Words (verbs) Cont.

seem	看上去	kàn shàng qù	**sign**	签名	qiān míng
seize	抓住	zhuā zhù	**sing**	唱	chàng
sell	卖	mài	**sleep**	睡觉	shuì jiào
send	送	sòng	**smoke**	吸烟	sī yān
separate	分开	fēn kāi	**snow**	下雪	xià xuě
serve	服务	fú wù	**speak**	发言	fā yán
set	放置	fàng zhì	**spend**	花	huā
sew	缝	féng	**thank**	感谢	gǎn xiè
shake	摇动	yáo dòng	**think**	想	xiǎng
shine	照耀	zhào yào	**throw**	扔	rēng
shout	喊	hǎn	**tire**	劳累	láo lèi
show	表示	biǎo shì	**touch**	触摸	chù mō

Action Words (verbs) Cont.

translate	翻译	fān yì	**want**	要	yào
travel	旅行	lǚ xíng	**wash**	洗	xǐ
try	试	shì	**watch**	观看	guān kàn
turn	转动	zhuàn dòng	**win**	赢	yíng
turn on	打开	dǎ kāi	**wish**	希望	xī wàng
turn off	关闭	guān bì	**work**	工作	gōng zuò
understand	懂	dǒng	**worry**	担心	dān xīn
use	用	yòng	**write**	写	xiě
visit	参观	cān guān	**wrestle**	摔跤	shuāi jiāo
vote	投票	tóu piào	**yawn**	打哈欠	dǎ hā qian
wait	等	děng			
walk	走	zǒu			

Where...?

năr

Where is/are...?	...zài năr?
Where am I?	Wǒ zài năr?
Where are we?	Wǒ men zài năr?
Where are you?	Nǐ zài năr?
Where do you live?	Nǐ zài năr zhù?
Where do you work?	Nǐ zài năr gōng zuò?
Where do you want to eat?	Nǐ xiǎng qù năr chī fàn?
Where are you from?	Nǐ cóng năr lái?
Where are you going?	Nǐ qù năr?
Where do you want to go?	Nǐ yào qù năr?
Where is the restroom?	Xǐ shǒu jiān zài năr?

When...?

shén me shí hòu

When does it leave?	Shén me shí hòu kāi?
When does it arrive?	Shén me shí hòu dào?
When does it start?	Shén me shí hòu kāi shǐ?
When does it finish?	Shén me shí hòu jié shù?
When does it return?	Shén me shí hòu huí lai?
When did this happen?	Shén me shí hòu fā shēng de?
When do you wan to eat?	Nǐ xiǎng shén me shí hòu qù chī fàn?
When will it be ready?	Shén me shí hòu hǎo?
When were you born?	Nǐ shì shén me shí hòu shēng de?
When is your birthday?	Shén me shí hòu shì nǐ de shēng rì?
When do you want it ?	Nǐ xiǎng shén me shí hòu yào?

Chinese does not have an equivalent of "it", which is often used
in English to represent things like the "flight", the "train", the
"movie", etc. In these circumstances, you need to mention the
word "the flight" and so on.

What...?
zěn me (yàng)

How are you?	Nǐ hǎo ma?
How do you say...?	... zěn me shuō?
How's it going?	Nǐ zěn me yàng?
How do you write it?	Zhè gè zì zěn me xiě?
How do you say it?	Zhè gè zěn me shuō?
How do you know?	Nǐ shì zěn me zhī dào de?
How do you want to pay?	Nín xiǎng zěn me fù qián?
I don't know how.	Wǒ bù zhī dào zěn me zuò.
How is your mother doing?	Nǐ de mā ma zěn me yàng?
How should I know?	Wǒ zěn me huì zhī dào?
How strange!	Zhēn qí guài!
How come you didn't go?	Nǐ zěn me méi qù?

How...?
shén me

What's this/that?	Zhè/nà shì shén me?
What does it mean?	Zhè shì shén me yì si?
What did you say?	Nǐ shuō shén me?
What's new?	Yǒu shén me xīn wén ma?
What's wrong?	Chū le shén me shì?
What are you doing?	Nǐ zài zuò shén me?
What do you want?	Nǐ yào shén me?
What's your name?	Nǐ jiào shén me?
What's your phone number?	Nǐ de diàn huà shì duō shǎo?
What's your address?	Nǐ de dì zhǐ shì shén me?
What time is it?	Jǐ diǎn le?
What's the date today?	Jīn tiān jǐ hào?

Which...?

nǎ yí (gè...)

Which one?	Nǎ yí gè?
Which ones?	Nǎ yì xiē?
Which one is yours?	Nǎ yí gè shì nǐ de?
Which one do you like?	Nǐ xǐ hua nǎ yí gè?
Which one is it?	Shì nǎ yí gè?
Which hotel?	Nǎ yí gè jiǔ diàn?
Which restaurant?	Nǎ yí gè fàn guǎn?
Which day?	Nǎ yì tiān?
Which seat is mine?	Nǎ yí gè zuò wèi shì wǒ de?
Which taxi is ours?	Nǎ yí gè chū zū chē shì wǒ men de?
Which airline?	Nǎ yí gè háng kōng gōng sī?
Which museum are we going to see?	
	Wǒ men yào qù nǎ yí gè bó wù guǎn?

How much...?
duō shǎo

How much is it?	Duō shǎo qián?
How much does it cost?	Zhè gè duō shǎo qián?
How much did you pay?	Nǐ fù le duō shǎo qián?
How much is it worth?	Zhè gè zhí duō shǎo qián?
How much time do we have?	Wǒ men yǒu duō shǎo shí jiān?
How much do I owe you?	Wǒ qiàn nǐ duō shǎo qián?
How many do you want?	Nǐ yào duō shǎo?
How many do you have?	Nǐ yǒu duō shǎo?
How many times?	Duō shǎo cì?
How many nights?	Duō shǎo gè wǎn shàng?
How many kids do you have?	Nǐ yǒu duō shǎo gè hái zi?
For how long?	Duō cháng shí jiān?

Portions & Measurements

A dozen	一打	yì dá	**inch**	英寸	yīng cùn
A gallon	一加仑	yì jiā lún	**centimeter**	厘米	lí mǐ
A handful	一把	yì bǎ	**foot**	英尺	yīng zhǐ
An ounce	一盎司	yí àng sī	**gallon**	加仑	jiā lún
A pair	一副	yí fù	**kilogram**	公斤	gōng jīn
A piece	一件	yí jiàn	**kilometer**	公里	gōng lǐ
A pint	一品脱	yì pǐn tuō	**liter**	升	shēng
A pound	一磅	yí bàng	**meter**	米	mǐ
A half mile	半英里	bàn yīng lǐ	**mile**	英里	yīng lǐ
A quart	夸脱	kuā tuō	**ounce**	盎司	àng sī
A slice	一片	yí piàn	**pound**	磅	bàng

241

Common Measurements

1 millimeter = .0400 inches
1 centimeter = .3940 inches
1 meter = 39.3700 inches
1 kilometer = 3,281.5 feet
1 kilometer = .621 miles

1 inch = 2.5400 centimeters
1 foot = 30.4800 centimeters
1 yard = 91.4400 centimeters
1 mile = 1.6090 kilometers

Metric Weight & Measures

1 liter = 1.057 quarts
1 liter = .264 gallon
3.785 liters = 1 gallon

1 ounce = 28.3500 grams
1 pound = 0.4540 kilograms
1 gram = .035 ounces

Inches to centimeters, multiply by 2.54
Centimeters to inches, multiply by .394